Animal Messengers

Brenda Parkes

People can talk.

People can write.

People have many ways to send messages.

U.S.MAIL

Animals are different. Some animals send messages by making sounds.

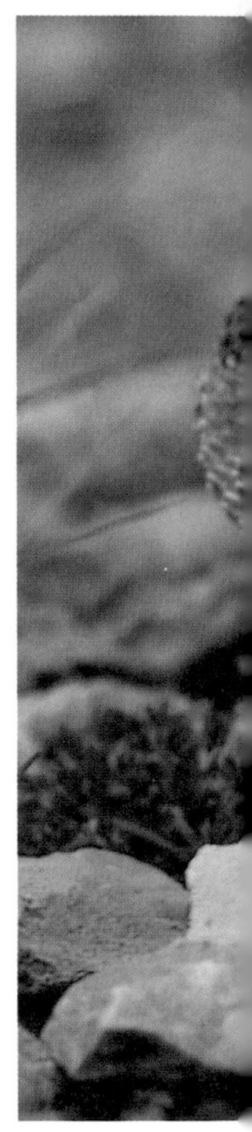

This snake shakes the rattle
on its tail.
The sound means, "Watch out!"

Some animals use signals
to send messages.
This bird signals, "Look at me!"

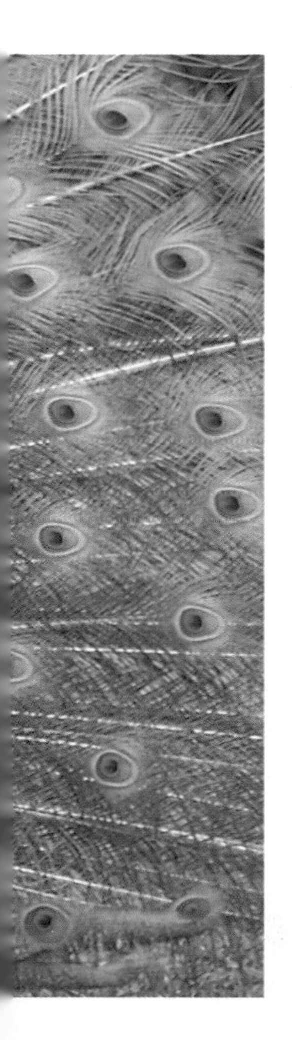

This deer flashes
its white tail.
This signal means,
"Danger!"

This bee is doing a dance.
This signal means,
"I know where to find food!"

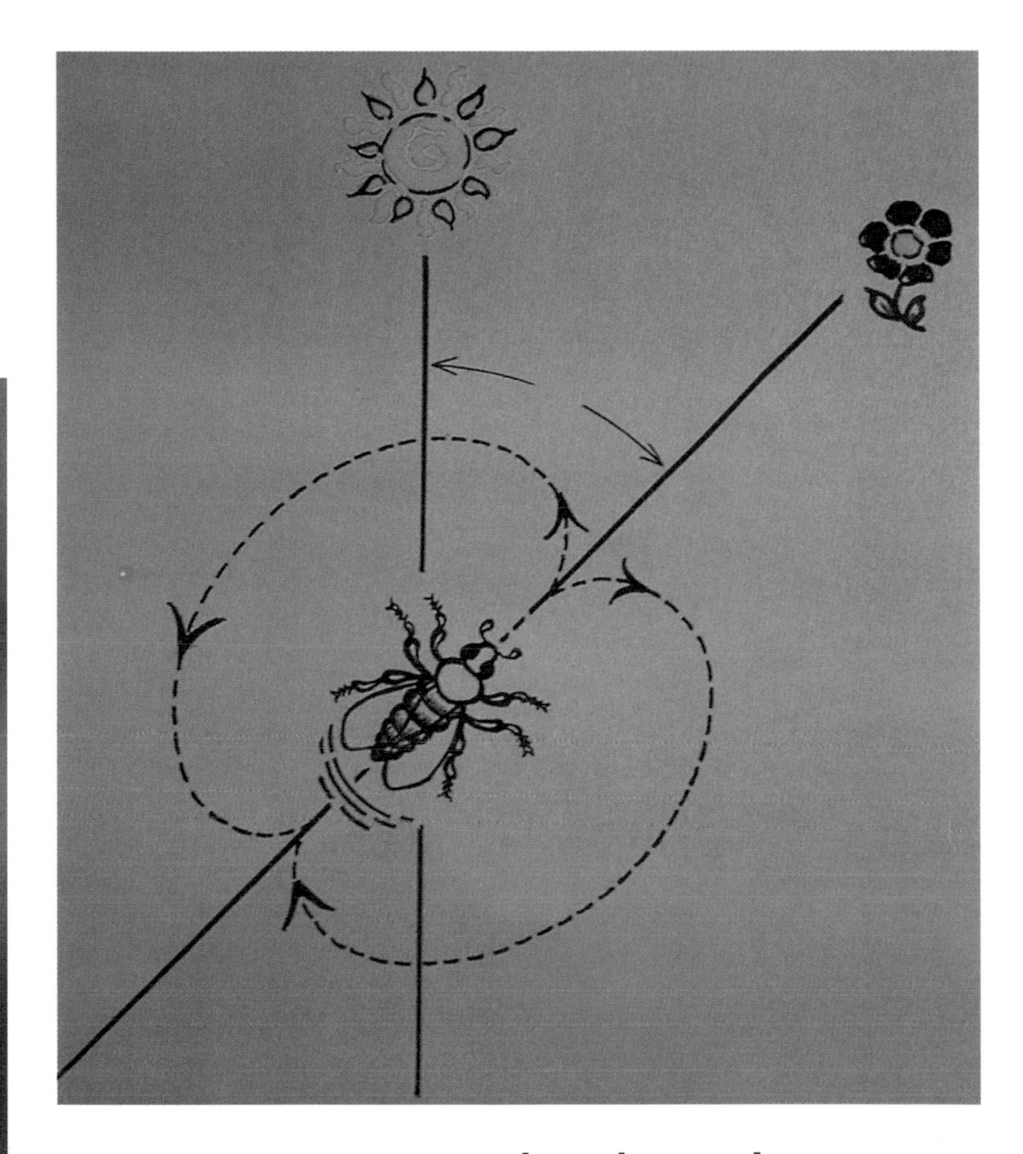

A scientist made this diagram to show how the bee dances.

Some animals send messages by touching.

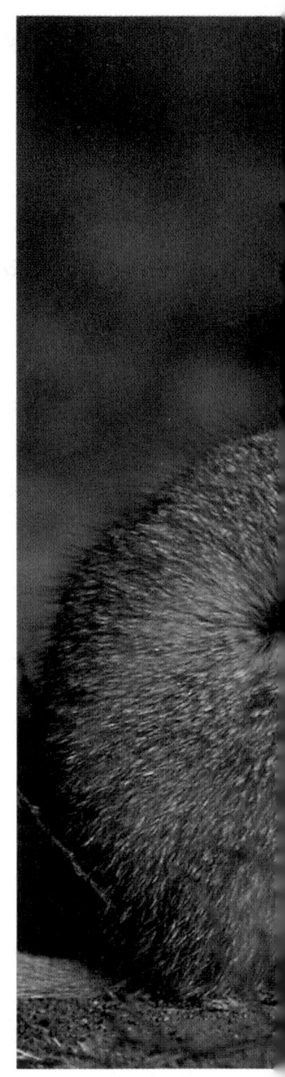

These prairie dogs touch noses.
This touch means, "Hello!"

My cat is telling me something.

I get the message!
It's time for her to eat.

Index